MONEY

Making Coins and Bills

Julie Haydon

A+
Smart Apple Media

This edition first published in 2006 in the United States of America by Smart Apple Media.

Smart Apple Media
2140 Howard Drive West
North Mankato
Minnesota 56003

First published in 2006 by
MACMILLAN EDUCATION AUSTRALIA PTY LTD
627 Chapel Street, South Yarra, Australia 3141

Visit our Web site at www.macmillan.com.au

Associated companies and representatives throughout the world.

Library of Congress Cataloging-in-Publication Data

Haydon, Julie.
  Making coins and bills / by Julie Haydon.
  p. cm. — (Money)
  ISBN-13: 978-1-58340-784-4
  1. Money—Juvenile literature. 2. Coinage--Juvenile literature. I. Title. II. Series.

  HG221.5.H393 2006
  737.40—dc22   2005057884

Edited by Miriana Dasovic
Text and cover design by Raul Diche
Page layout by Raul Diche
Photo research by Legend Images
Illustrations by Ann Likhovetsky

Printed in USA

Acknowledgments
The author wishes to thank the following people for their assistance with the preparation of the manuscript: Steve Pearce, Vivienne Thom and Thomas Firth from the Royal Australian Mint, Shrivalli Nanduri from Note Printing Australia; Mark Worby from the Reserve Bank of Australia, and the Bureau of Engraving and Printing in the USA.

The author and the publisher are grateful to the following for permission to reproduce copyright material:

Cover photograph: Man making coin blanks, courtesy of Australian Picture Library/Corbis; background image courtesy of Photodisc.

Australian Picture Library/Corbis, pp. 7, 8, 10, 13, 23, 24, 25, 26, 29; Bureau of Engraving and Printing, United States Department of the Treasury, p. 9; Coo-ee Historical Picture Library, p. 18 (bottom); Mark Nolan/Getty Images, p. 27; U.S. Bureau of Engraving and Printing/Getty Images, p. 21; © Jane Sweeney, Lonely Planet Images, p. 6; MEA Photo, p. 18 (top); National Australia Bank, p. 4 (bottom); Photodisc, pp. 3, 4 (top left), 30, 32; Photolibrary/ Reso E.E.I.G, p. 5; Photoobjects, © 2005 JupiterImages Corporation, p. 19 (top); Photos.com, pp. 4 (top right), 19 (bottom); Reserve Bank of Australia, pp. 14, 15, 16, 17, 20, 28; Royal Australian Mint, p. 22.

Contents

Glossary words

When a word is printed in **bold**, you can look up its meaning in the glossary on page 31.

Money

Most people use money every day. Money is what we use to pay for things. There are different forms of money. Coins and bills are forms of money, but people can also pay for things with **credit cards** and **checks**. Some people pay for things with the money they have in bank accounts. People can move money in and out of their bank accounts electronically.

Using money

Money is used to buy **products**, such as food and clothes, and to pay for **services**, such as electricity, or a visit to the dentist. Money is also used to pay **debts**, and to store wealth, which means that money can be put away and used later.

Info-plus!

Most countries have their own type of money. A type of money is called a currency.

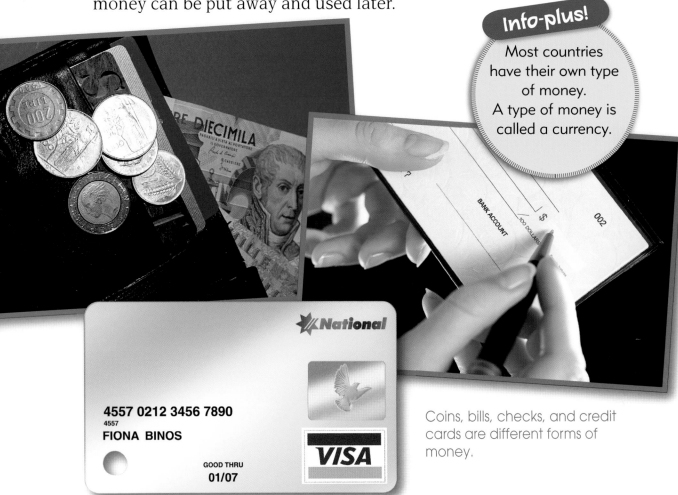

Coins, bills, checks, and credit cards are different forms of money.

4

Coins and bills

Coins and bills are convenient forms of money, because they are easy to carry and easy to use. Coins and bills are made from materials such as metal, paper, and plastic. They need to be hard-wearing because they are handled by lots of people and by machines, such as vending machines and **automatic teller machines**, or **ATMs**.

Coins and bills are also called cash. Many people use cash when they are paying for small purchases.

Governments

Governments make coins and bills. They decide what the coins and bills will be made from, what they will look like, and how many will be made. Most coins and bills are made from cheap materials. Their worth comes from the **value** that a government gives each coin and bill, not from the materials used to make them. People accept this value, and use coins and bills to make and receive payments.

Cash is often used to pay for inexpensive goods.

Money through time

Long ago, people did not use money. They hunted and gathered food and materials, and made simple tools. If a person had something another person wanted, the two people bartered. This means they exchanged products and services for other products and services, without using money.

Later, when people began to settle in villages, products such as farm animals, salt, and shells became very popular for bartering. These products became the first types of money.

In some parts of the world, people still barter animals, instead of using money.

Metal money

Over time, people realized that metal as money had many advantages over other products as money. Metal money was easy to transport, weigh, divide, count, and store. It was accepted in most places, and it lasted a long time.

The first types of metal money were unstamped pieces of metal. The size or shape of a piece of metal money was not important, because its value depended on its weight.

Coins

The first coins were made during the 600s B.C. They were a fixed weight, and were stamped with designs to show their value. The coins were made from electrum, which is a natural mixture of gold and silver. Later, coins were made from pure gold and pure silver.

Modern coins are made from cheap metals. The **face value** of a modern coin is greater than the value of its metal. The government that **issues** a modern coin decides its value.

Bills

Paper money has been used for more than a thousand years. Early forms of paper money were **receipts**. People left coins and **precious metals** with merchants and banks, and were given receipts. These receipts could be used to pay for products and services, and to pay debts. Modern bills are not receipts. The value of modern bills is based on trust. Everyone, including the issuing government, is supposed to accept them as money.

These ancient electrum coins, found in Turkey, were probably made in the 600s B.C.

Mints and bill printers

Coins are made at mints. Bills are printed at bill printers. Most mints and bill printers are owned by governments. It is expensive to build and operate these buildings, so some governments have their coins and bills made in other countries.

Mints

Mints are large, secure buildings that contain the machines and materials used to make coins. Many people work there. Mints make coins for daily use, called circulating coins. Most mints also make other items, such as coins for collectors, coins to celebrate special events, medals, and jewelry. Some mints also store precious metals.

Minting

Minting is the process of stamping blank pieces of metal with designs to make coins. The designs are **engraved** on metal tools, called dies. The dies are used in pairs, and hit both sides of a blank piece of metal at the same time. New dies are made for each new coin design.

This man is checking the quality of the copper used to make euro coins.

Info-plus!

Mints melt old and damaged coins, and use the metal to make new coins.

Bill printers

Bill printers are large, secure buildings that contain the machines and materials used to make bills. Many people work there. Bill printers print bills for daily use, called currency bills. Many bill printers also print other items, such as stamps, passports, and government invitations.

Printing

Printing is the process of copying words, numbers, and pictures onto materials such as paper, cloth, plastic, and metal. All the printed copies look the same. Modern printing machines can print many copies of an original quickly.

Paper or plastic bills

Modern bills are printed on paper or on a type of plastic, called polymer. Large blank sheets of the paper or plastic go through various printing machines at a bill printer to become bills.

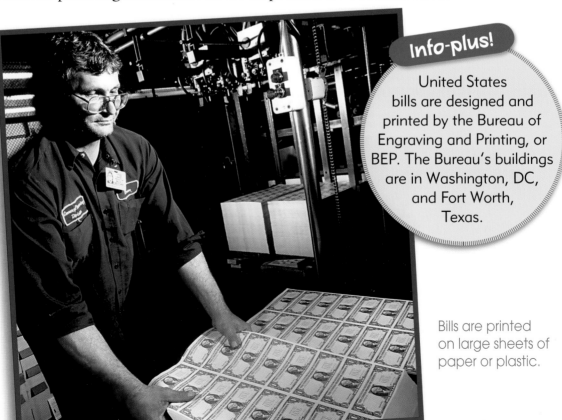

Info-plus!

United States bills are designed and printed by the Bureau of Engraving and Printing, or BEP. The Bureau's buildings are in Washington, DC, and Fort Worth, Texas.

Bills are printed on large sheets of paper or plastic.

Minting coins

Coins are made, or minted, at mints. Coins must be hard-wearing and light enough to carry easily. They must also be easy to recognize as money, but difficult to copy.

The planning

Planning is necessary before a new coin can be minted. First, the theme of the coin is chosen. The size, weight, material, color and shape of the coin must be decided. Then the designs for both sides of the coin are approved by the government.

The designs

Artists make large drawings of the designs. The designs are usually images from the issuing country, such as people, animals, plants, or buildings. Coin designs must also include the name of the issuing country, the **denomination** of the coin, and the year it was minted.

The side of a coin that bears the main design is called the obverse. The other side is called the reverse.

Blank pieces of metal are checked to make sure that they are the correct size, shape, and weight.

The clay model

A large model of the coin is made in clay. The model is much larger than the coin will be. An artist called a sculptor uses hand tools to cut the fine details of the designs into the clay. Later, more models of the coin are made in a variety of materials.

The dies

A special machine transfers the designs from the final model onto hard pieces of metal. These pieces of metal are the dies. The dies are put into a machine called a coining press. The coining press is used to stamp the designs onto the coins.

The blanks

Coins are made from blank pieces of metal, called blanks. A machine called a blanking press cuts the blanks from strips of metal. Most blanks are round, because most coins are round. The blanks are heated, cooled, washed, and dried. They go into an upsetting machine, which creates a rim around the edges of the blanks. Then the blanks go into the coining press.

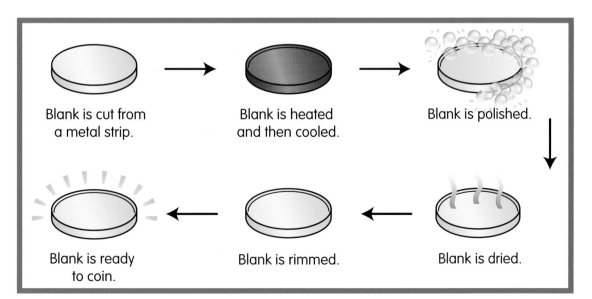

Blank is cut from a metal strip.

Blank is heated and then cooled.

Blank is polished.

Blank is dried.

Blank is rimmed.

Blank is ready to coin.

Stages in blank preparation.

The coining press

The coining press is used to stamp the designs onto the blanks. In the coining press, both sides of the blanks are hit by dies at the same time. This stamps the obverse and reverse designs onto the metal, and turns the blanks into coins.

The coins

After they have been stamped, the coins are checked and counted. They are put into bags that are weighed. The bags of coins are safely stored at the mint until they are transported to banks.

Early coins

Early coins were made by hand. The designs were engraved onto a piece of bronze or iron. This was the die. The die was fitted into a large metal block called an anvil. The coin blank was placed on top of the die. A thin rod called a punch was placed on the blank and then hit with a hammer. The punch made a mark in the blank while the other side of the blank was pressed into the die and marked with the design. This created a coin.

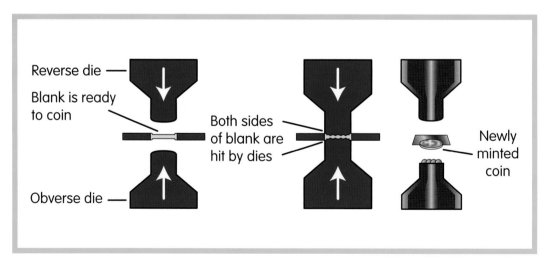

Stages in the coining press.

How coins are minted

Designing the dies

The theme for the coin is chosen.

↓

The designs for the coin are drawn.

↓

Large models of the coin are made.

↓

The dies are made.

↓

The dies are put into the coining press.

Making the blanks

The blanking press cuts blanks from strips of metal.

↓

The blanks are heated, cooled, washed, polished, and dried.

↓

The blanks go into the upsetting machine.

↓

The upsetting machine raises a rim around the edges of the blanks.

↓

The blanks go into the coining press.

At the coining press

In the coining press, both sides of the blanks are hit by dies at the same time. This makes coins.

↓

The new coins are checked and counted.

↓

The coins are put into bags that are weighed.

↓

The bags of coins are safely stored until they are transported to banks.

After they have been pressed, the coins are pushed into a machine that automatically counts them.

Printing bills

Bills are printed at a bill printer. Bills feature attractive designs that make them easy to recognize as money, but difficult to copy. Bills are often folded and crumpled in wallets and pockets, so they must be hard-wearing.

The planning

Planning is necessary before a new bill can be printed. First, the theme of the bill is chosen. The theme must be approved before the designs for both sides of the bill are chosen.

The designs

Artists make large drawings of the designs. The designs usually include images from the issuing country, patterns, colors, various security features, the name of the issuing country and other words, the denomination of the note, and a **serial number**.

Designs for the $100 bill are engraved onto a metal die.

The dies

Skilled artists called engravers use hand tools to cut, or engrave, the designs into pieces of metal. These metal pieces are the dies.

The printing plates

The designs on the dies are transferred to several different printing plates. The printing plates are put into several different printing machines.

The printing machines

The different printing machines contain inks and various printing plates. Bills are printed on sheets of paper or polymer. Dozens of bills are printed on one sheet. A sheet of paper or polymer must go through all the different printing machines in order for all the features of the bill to be printed on it.

Info-plus!

When the printing process is finished, the sheet of paper or polymer is a sheet of bills.

This printing press can print up to 8,000 bill sheets per hour, because it prints on both sides of the sheet at the same time.

Cutting the sheets

The sheets of bills are cut by a guillotine machine into individual bills.

Counting the bills

The bills are put into containers and counted by a machine. Damaged or poorly printed bills are removed.

The bills

The bills are wrapped, then safely stored at the printer until they are transported to banks.

Guillotine machines can cut through 100 sheets of bills at a time.

Info-plus!

United States bills do not feature the portraits of living people.

How bills are printed

Bills are printed on huge printing machines at a bill printer. The process is shown below.

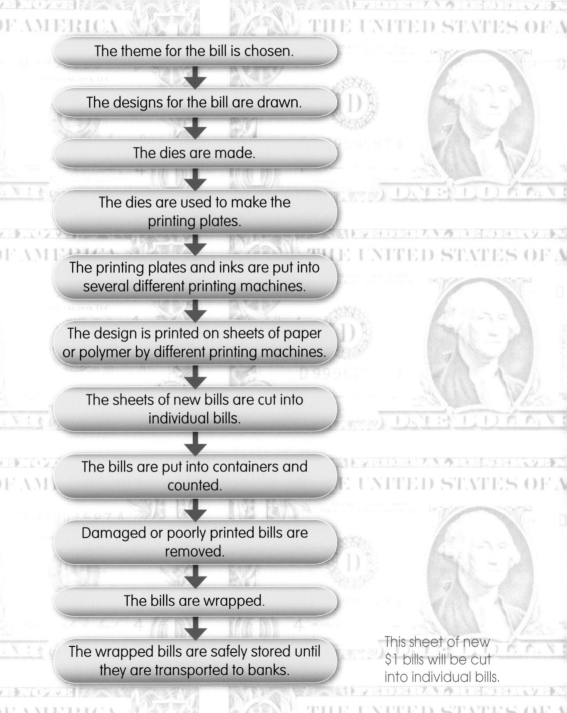

The theme for the bill is chosen.

↓

The designs for the bill are drawn.

↓

The dies are made.

↓

The dies are used to make the printing plates.

↓

The printing plates and inks are put into several different printing machines.

↓

The design is printed on sheets of paper or polymer by different printing machines.

↓

The sheets of new bills are cut into individual bills.

↓

The bills are put into containers and counted.

↓

Damaged or poorly printed bills are removed.

↓

The bills are wrapped.

↓

The wrapped bills are safely stored until they are transported to banks.

This sheet of new $1 bills will be cut into individual bills.

Portraits of the famous

The portraits of many famous people are featured on coins and bills all over the world. People are usually chosen to appear on a country's coins and bills because they have done something special for that country.

George Washington

George Washington is featured on the United States $1 bill. Between 1775 and 1783, George Washington was the leader of the American army that successfully fought the British during the American Revolution. In 1789, George Washington became the first President of the United States. He played an important role in uniting the country and in creating the constitution, or the rules used to govern the country.

George Washington (1732–1799)

Sir John A. Macdonald

Sir John A. Macdonald is featured on the Canadian $10 bill. He was Canada's first Prime Minister, from 1867 to 1873. Sir John A. Macdonald played an important role in uniting Canada, and in building a railway line across the country.

Sir John A. Macdonald (1815–1891)

Her Majesty Queen Elizabeth II

Her Majesty Queen Elizabeth II is featured on the reverse of Australia's coins and on the front of the Australian $5 bill. The queen lives in England. She is the symbolic head of Australia, which means that she does not have an active role in governing Australia.

Her Majesty Queen Elizabeth II (1926–) is printed on the reverse of all Australian coins.

Sir Edmund Hillary

Sir Edmund Hillary is featured on New Zealand's $5 bill. Sir Edmund is a famous mountain-climber and explorer. In 1953, he became the first person to climb the world's highest mountain, Mount Everest. Five years later, Sir Edmund was the first person to drive across Antarctica to the South Pole.

Sir Edmund Hillary (1919–)

Security features

Only governments are allowed to make and issue coins and bills. To stop people making illegal copies, called counterfeits, coins and bills include various security features. Security features are easy to check, but difficult to copy without the proper materials and equipment.

United States' $20 bill

Some of the security features on this bill are shown below.

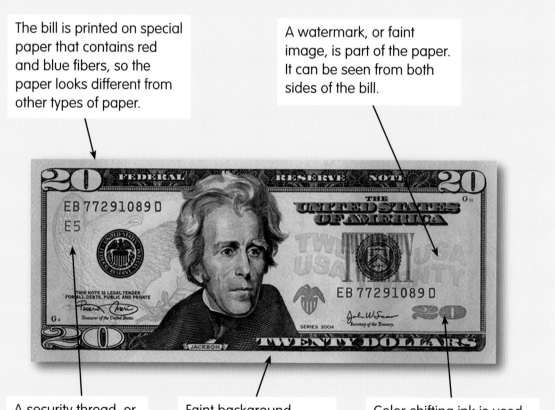

The bill is printed on special paper that contains red and blue fibers, so the paper looks different from other types of paper.

A watermark, or faint image, is part of the paper. It can be seen from both sides of the bill.

A security thread, or plastic strip, is in the paper. This can be seen when the bill is held to the light.

Faint background colors are printed on the bill. Without the proper inks and printing machines, these are hard to copy.

Color-shifting ink is used to print the number 20 in the lower right corner. When the bill is moved, the color-shifting ink changes color.

Check your money

It is difficult and expensive for counterfeiters to make coins and bills that look and feel like real money. Most counterfeiters cannot copy security features well, so it is a good idea to check the security features on your money.

Australia's $20 bill

Some of the security features on this bill are shown below.

The bill is printed on polymer. It does not feel like paper, or tear easily like paper.

A shadow image of Australia's coat-of-arms, the shield with a kangaroo and an emu, appears under light.

Intaglio print is a raised print that can be felt by running a finger over the bill. It is used for portraits and some other design elements.

The clear window is part of the bill, not added on. It contains an image of a compass with **embossing** of the number 20.

When the see-through registration device is seen under a light, a star with seven points is visible. Four of the points are on one side of the bill, and the other three points are on the other side.

Security at mints and bill printers

Newly made coins and bills must be kept safe from thieves. The designs, materials, and equipment used to make coins and bills must also be protected from theft. This is why mints and bill printers have high levels of security.

The buildings

Mints and bill printers are housed in buildings that are made from concrete or other strong materials. The buildings are often built on slabs of concrete or rock to stop thieves from tunnelling in. Tall security fences surround the buildings.

Security staff

Security staff play an important role in protecting mints and bill printers. They patrol the grounds 24 hours a day, and check and operate security equipment. They also watch over staff and visitors, to stop them stealing money and equipment.

The buildings of the U.S. Mint in Denver are protected by strong fences.

Security equipment

Mints and bill printers are fitted with security equipment, such as cameras, alarms, special computers, and complicated locks. Staff must use identity cards to enter the building.

Vaults

Vaults are secure rooms for storing valuables. They have heavy metal doors, and security locks and alarms. Newly made coins and bills are stored in vaults at mints and bill printers until it is time for them to be transported to banks.

Armored trucks

Newly made coins and bills are transported from mints and bill printers to banks in armored trucks. The trucks contain guards, who unload and carry the money into the banks.

Info-plus!

Security is tight at mints and bill printers, but thefts still occur. Between 1993 and 2002, the Bureau of Engraving and Printing reported thefts by staff of about $1.8 million.

Newly made coins and bills are stored in vaults.

Jobs at mints and bill printers

Many people work at mints and bill printers. It is important, skilled work. Here are some of the jobs that people do.

Artists

Artists make drawings of the designs that will appear on coins and bills. The drawings are large, so that all the fine details of the designs can be shown. If a portrait is to be included in the design, an artist will often refer to photographs of the person portrayed. This helps the artist to draw the portrait. It is common for a different artist to design each side of a coin or bill.

Sculptors

Sculptors use the artists' drawings to make clay models of coins. A sculptor then carefully cuts the designs into the clay. The model has to be much larger than the coin, so that the sculptor can include all the fine details.

A sculptor cuts the designs into a large clay model of the coin.

Engravers

Engravers use the artists' drawings to make metal dies. The dies are used to make the printing plates for bills. Engravers cut the bill designs onto the pieces of metal. The designs must be engraved back-to-front on the dies in order to be printed facing the right way. Engravers work by hand, using sharp tools.

Machine operators

Machine operators work the various machines found at mints and bill printers. Machine operators check that their machines are working properly. If not, the operator has to report the fault so that it can be fixed quickly. Modern machines can operate without much human help. For example, one person can operate a bagging machine that can package up to two million circulating coins in one day.

Info-plus!

The original metal dies that are used to make coins and bills are carefully stored, so that they can be used again if needed.

This man operates a machine used to make euro blanks.

25

Inspectors

Trained inspectors check newly made coins and bills for flaws. They remove any coins and bills that are damaged or poorly made. These coins and bills are destroyed. If necessary, the dies and printing plates used to make the flawed coins and bills are removed and checked.

Tour guides

Some mints and bill printers offer tours. Tour guides lead visitors through the buildings. People on the tour watch coins or bills being made, while the tour guide explains the steps and answers questions. Some buildings display old equipment as well as old coins and bills, and a tour guide explains their history. Many tour guides end the tour at a shop on the premises, where people can buy souvenirs, such as collector coins or bills.

On some tours, visitors who cannot hear well can ask for a tour guide who knows sign language.

Newly printed bills are inspected to check that they have no flaws.

Office staff

Many people work in offices at mints and bill printers. There are accountants, who take care of the finances. There are marketing people, who tell the media and public about new products and events. There are staff whose work is to order materials, such as strips of metal for coin blanks, and inks for the printing machines. Some staff do administrative work, such as typing and photocopying.

Sales staff

Sales staff work in a mint's or bill printer's shop selling various products. Customers can also order items over the Internet, or by phone, or fax. Many serious collectors buy collector coins or sheets of bills from these shops. Sales staff must know their products well, so that they can answer questions from customers.

Shops at mints and bill printers sell a wide range of goods.

Mints and bill printers in the future

In the future, mints and bill printers will use new designs, materials and machines to make new series of coins and bills. New series of coins and bills are issued from time to time, to make it difficult for counterfeiters to keep up with the changes.

Designs

In the future, new designs will be created for coins and bills. Artists already use computers to create and design parts. Future designs may be created entirely on computers and have more complicated parts. The more detailed a design is, the harder it is to copy.

Materials

In the future, new materials will be invented that can be used to make coins and bills even more secure from counterfeiting. The new materials will also have to be long-lasting, light to carry, recyclable, and easy to mint or print.

Old polymer bills are recycled by being turned into granules and used to make plastic products, such as compost bins.

Machines

In the future, mints and bill printers will be fitted with the latest machines. These will include new computers, new printing and minting machines, and new security systems. These machines will help to make the jobs easier and faster, improve the security features on coins and bills, and make the buildings more secure. Mints and bill printers must use new equipment as it becomes available, so that they can stay ahead of counterfeiters and thieves.

The future of cash

Fewer coins and bills may be produced in the future, as more people make payments with other forms of money. It is likely that many payments in the future will be made electronically, so less cash will be required.

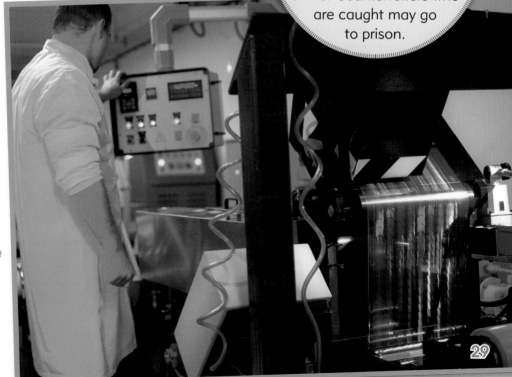

Info-plus!

Today, counterfeiters sometimes use machines such as inkjet printers, color photocopiers, and scanners to copy paper bills. This is a crime. Counterfeiters who are caught may go to prison.

This man is operating a machine that prints high-tech holograms, which is a design feature that makes bills difficult to counterfeit.

Start a coin collection

You can start your own coin collection.

You will need:

- coins
- a coin album
- a pencil

What to do:

1 Decide what sort of coins to collect. Some collectors collect coins from one country, while others collect coins from many countries. You may want to collect only one denomination of coins, coins minted in a certain year, or coins with designs that fit a theme.

2 Collect your first coins. You can ask friends and family to collect circulating coins for you when they travel to other countries. You can also buy coins from mints, coin shops, or coin fairs.

3 Display your coins in a coin album. Write the name of the issuing country and the year of issue next to the coin.

4 Read books and Web sites about coins.

Info-plus!

The study or collection of coins is called numismatics.

Coin collecting is a hobby enjoyed by people of all ages.

Glossary

automatic teller machines or ATMs machines used by customers with a banking card, to withdraw money or do other banking

checks printed forms used instead of cash, with instructions telling a bank who and how much to pay

credit cards pieces of plastic that have numbers, names, a signature, and a magnetic stripe on them

debts money owed

denomination the value shown on a coin or bill

embossing a technique that creates raised patterns on materials such as paper and plastic

engraved when words or designs are cut into metal

face value the value shown on a coin or bill

issues gives out, distributes

precious metals valuable metals, such as gold and silver

products objects that are bought, sold, or bartered

receipts special notes that prove someone has received money or products, or that someone has bought something

serial number an individual number printed on a bill for identification

services work that people pay others to do or provide

value the worth of something

Index